A MIND SHAPED BY POVERTY

◆

Ten Things Educators Should Know

Regenia Rawlinson

iUniverse, Inc.
Bloomington

A Mind Shaped by Poverty
Ten Things Educators Should Know

iUniverse Star
an iUniverse, Inc. imprint

iUniverse books may be ordered through booksellers or by contacting:

iUniverse
1663 Liberty Drive
Bloomington, IN 47403
www.iuniverse.com
1-800-Authors (1-800-288-4677)

ISBN: 978-1-936236-71-8 (sc)
ISBN: 978-1-936236-72-5 (e)

Library of Congress Control Number: 2011908299

Printed in the United States of America

iUniverse rev. date: 7/29/2011

To my husband David, my best friend and strongest advocate, and my children David, Bradford, and Brittany, who taught me more about myself than I thought I needed to learn. They also taught me how to recognize the important things in life. They are my inspiration and my joy. I am very proud of them.

Contents

Preface. ix

Acknowledgments. xi

Introduction. xiii

CHAPTER 1.   Fairness 1

CHAPTER 2.   Access .3

CHAPTER 3.   Scarcity 6

CHAPTER 4.   Protest. 8

CHAPTER 5.   Entitlement 11

CHAPTER 6.   Second-Rate. 14

CHAPTER 7.   Escape from Stress. 16

CHAPTER 8.   Discretionary Learning 18

CHAPTER 9.   Haphazard Assembly 20

CHAPTER 10.   Options 23

CHAPTER 11.   More Suggestions 26

CHAPTER 12.   Behaviors and Feelings 28

CHAPTER 13.   Teacher Perception Is Important. 30

CHAPTER 14.   Keeping Expectations High 32

Conclusion 33

Bibliography. 35

About the Author 37

Preface

This is the first of two books. Each explores ten phenomena to help teachers understand how poverty can shape a child's mind. Personal stories illustrate each of the ten, and at the end of each story, I suggest strategies to help overcome a poverty mindset. I hope this book will help teachers grasp the pervasive, negative effects that living in poverty has on a child's mind.

Acknowledgments

I acknowledge the difficulty students from poverty face daily at school. They must learn a new system of knowing and learning, which can be confusing and frustrating at times.

Introduction

I grew up in a home with sixteen siblings. I was the seventh child. My parents were sharecroppers who farmed tobacco, corn, cotton, wheat, and cucumbers to earn money to support the family. I lived in poverty. My family had limited financial resources for clothing, household items, and food. My house leaked when it rained because there were holes in the roof. Rats, snakes, spiders, water bugs, and other insects whose names I do not know found their way into our home through holes and broken windows. My parents could afford indoor plumbing only years after I left home, benefiting the four youngest. When I entered school, I took all the pain, anger, frustration, resentment, shame, low self-esteem, debilitating worldview, and dehumanizing effects of poverty with me. I had a poverty mind-set.

Many students in poverty have spotty-to-poor academic records that can often be linked to the poverty mind-set that strips students of ambition and enthusiasm and makes them indifferent. Students with a poverty mind-set often feel powerless and think they have no control over what happens in their lives. They blame their circumstances and other people and look to others to work things out for them. They attribute failure to their lack of ability rather than their deficient work. In some ways, I was much like them.

Helping such students create a record of good grades of which they can be proud is this book's primary goal. I call the collective effects of poverty the *scourge of poverty* because of the plaguing consequences. Poverty shapes the mind for self-sabotage and possibly for self-destruction. Poverty makes people think they are unworthy. People who grow up in poverty accept and record the message of unworthiness and play the recording wherever they go. The tape plays, and they act out the message. Counterproductive behaviors in the classroom may be evidence of the message. When I reflect on my school experiences, I realize that by failing to complete homework assignments and not turning in class assignments, I sabotaged my chances of high academic achievement.

The confidence students need to succeed in the classroom is linked to the message recorded in their minds. I recorded a message of inadequacy that played every time I attempted new things. In many cases, I gave up before I really tried. Recording a message of worthiness can help students gain the confidence they need. I wonder if I would have accomplished more had I recorded a positive message. Teachers can help students record a new message of worthiness by what and how they communicate.

My hope is that this book will give teachers guidance when they confront the scourge of poverty. A poverty mind-set has left many in frustrating and unproductive lives. I trust we can keep that from happening to the students in our charge.

The Crisis. The poverty rate varies from state to state. According to the United Health Foundation[1], the number of children living in poverty has increased in twenty-five states, while other states showed a decrease. Minnesota has the lowest poverty rate, and Mississippi tops the list with the highest poverty rate.

The U.S. Census Bureau[2] reports that 16.7 percent of all children under eighteen live in poverty. According to Focus Adolescent Services[3], nearly half the heads of households on welfare are dropouts. In 2002, the U.S. Census Bureau fixed the poverty rate for children living in single-parent homes headed by a female at 26.5 percent, compared to 5.3 percent for children living in married-couple homes. Children raised in single-parent homes are more likely to live below the poverty level than children in two-parent homes are. For many of those children, education could be a way out of poverty.

Education is a critical factor in economic success. According to the United Health Foundation, high school graduation rates dropped from 72.9 percent in 1990 to 68.3 percent in 2005. They also report that fewer than 60 percent of incoming ninth graders graduate in four years. Focus Adolescent Services suggests that recent high school graduates will earn significantly less than college graduates, "in their lifetime." Movement into an information-based economy increases the demand for more highly skilled workers. Dropouts will not be able to compete for job opportunities that could help them escape poverty. That could result in another generation with little chance of a life of economic prosperity.

---

1   United Health Foundation, *16ᵗʰ Annual America's Health Rankings Shows Slowing Rate of Improvement after Significant Health Gains in 1990s*, (pages 1–5).

2   U.S. Census Bureau, *Poverty: 2002 Highlights*, (pages 1 & 2).

3   Focus Adolescent Services, *Youth Who Drop Out*, (page 3).

The Challenge. Many students living in poverty enter school with barriers that interfere with learning and make it more difficult for them to stay in school. In addition to being from single-parent homes, many are unready for school[4], lack proper medical care, and have a poverty mindset, all obstacles to staying in school. The poverty mindset is one of the most difficult and pervasive challenges to overcome. Years of interaction with the environment of poverty contribute to the development of that mindset, and it does not discriminate. It can plague all races, religions, and national origins. No one who lives or has lived in poverty is exempt.

A poverty mindset can infiltrate the classroom and instigate or mask destructive and self-defeating behaviors that frustrate teachers, whose efforts to eliminate them often fail. Students sense their frustration and respond with resentment. The child labels the teacher insensitive and uncaring. The teacher accuses the student of disrespect and a nasty attitude. Feeling victimized, many of those students drop out of school. Some become involved in high-risk behaviors and show up in the familiar statistics. They may be imprisoned, abuse drugs, or join the welfare rolls. The long-term impact could be a life of crime or stagnation in a low-wage job.

While the long-term impact is frightening, the short-term implications are also urgent. Many frustrated students fall behind their peers academically, and yet the school systems retain them. Repeated retention generates more frustration and discouragement. Disruptive or destructive behaviors are predictable human responses to discouragement. Exclusion from school by suspension or expulsion is probable. Without intervention, the cycle of failure and exclusion repeats itself.

Confronting the poverty mindset can counteract long-and short-term negative impacts, and the challenge for educators is to help students overcome this barrier to foster success in the classroom. As a snotty-nosed and crudely dressed student, I found teachers did not aggressively support my success in the classroom. They were not outwardly discouraging, but they were noticeably aloof. I needed my teachers to understand the poverty mindset (which was my situation) and encourage me. Their understanding and encouragement would have given me badly needed support in the classroom and would have ultimately contributed to my success.

After more than thirty years of experience working with educators, I have concluded that many of my teachers lacked the skills and training to address my unique needs, as do many today. Many were from a middle-class background and did not understand what living in poverty meant. Teachers

---

4   Saluja, Scott-Little, and Clifford, *Readiness for School: A Survey of State Policies and Definitions*, (pages 1–14).

can benefit from professional development to help them understand students raised in poverty, the mindset they bring with them, and the techniques and strategies that promote achievement.

The Scourge of Poverty and Why I Wrote This Book. Poverty profoundly affected what I came to believe about myself and what I accepted for my life and future. To help readers understand the power the scourge of poverty wields over a life, how it infiltrates all aspects, I will share some of the mindset I formed while I lived in poverty. Although I left the poverty environment physically, I still struggle daily to escape the mindset of poverty.

I will attempt to illustrate the role the scourge of poverty plays in the classroom. Disruptive, aggressive, lethargic, and angry behaviors often mask the scourge of poverty. When a student living in poverty behaves in counterproductive ways, one must pause and ask why. This does not suggest or condone making excuses, but rather seeks the underlying reasons for such behaviors. Understanding why the students misbehave can lead to strategies for help.

My goal here is to paint a picture of poverty that readers can understand intellectually and connect with emotionally. After all, children who live in poverty are human and want the same things other children want—to be treated with respect and given equal opportunities, though they may ask for them differently. What they believe about themselves and their lives determines how they ask. I share some things I believed about myself and about my life after living in poverty, show how these beliefs could be true for others living in poverty situations, and suggest how they may play out in the classroom. Finally, I offer strategies for educators to help students overcome the effects of a poverty mindset.

1

✦

Fairness

I BELIEVED THAT LIFE was not fair and would never be fair to me. I could not understand why certain people in Trio, the small town in South Carolina where I lived, had so much more than we did. We worked long and hard while they seemingly did nothing, yet they drove the cars, had the pools, and lived in nice homes. They had air conditioning. I dreamed of what living in such a home must have been like. My home did not have air conditioning, and a pool was not even on my radar screen of hope.

My parents sharecropped for a time with a wealthy man in Trio whose identity I will protect by calling him *Mr. Ed.* Sharecropping meant that one partner supplied the financing, and the other supplied the labor. My father supplied the labor. At the end of the farming season, the two partners totaled all expenses and supposedly divided the profits equally. My father always ended the year in debt to Mr. Ed. I could not understand it then, and I still do not know how it could be possible. After all, my father's many children worked, while Mr. Ed. had no one in the fields. If my father could be treated unfairly and was powerless to do anything about it, what power could I ever have? This scary thought ballooned into distrust and skepticism of certain people. Other sharecroppers told the same story when they visited my father, so I decided that fairness was not in the cards if you belonged to a certain class of people.

Children who grow up witnessing unfairness learn to distrust those who act unfairly: an ethnic group, perhaps, or a socioeconomic class, or people living in certain neighborhoods. The results are the same. When they come to school, children immediately categorize students and educators, especially teachers, into groups. They need to know whom they can trust and who warrants skepticism. Their experiences guide them and inform their decisions about who goes into what group. They distinguish others by their skin color,

1

behavior, language, hairstyle, clothing, interaction with others, and food. Children of poverty are very adept at detecting unfairness, since they have seen it often and in numerous forms. When it shows up in the school or the classroom, directly or indirectly, it confirms what they already believe. In the new school environment, they meet unfairness in numerous places. Distrustful and skeptical, they reject the help of anyone in the suspect group, even though the person extending the help may be falsely marked. They turn away from the help because of the group likeness. In the tug-of-war that results, they will do nothing they think satisfies a perceived antagonist, even if that means hurting themselves. All they want is to get even. They want you to feel what they feel.

If they mark a teacher as belonging to a group they perceive as unfair, students will initially reject that teacher's assistance. The rejection may be masked by refusal to complete assignments, sleeping, abrasive responses, and disruptive behaviors. They will not trust teachers to grade fairly and will register complaints about unfair treatment related to discipline.

Ross's story illustrates this point well. Ross, an eleventh grade student, stormed into my office. He was furious with the teacher for referring him to the assistant principal for sleeping in class. Ross admits dozing off in class and he insists everyone sleeps in class but he is the only student the teacher sends to the office for discipline.

Consistent treatment for all students can arrest the attitude of distrust and skepticism. The students' attitude toward the antagonist group as a whole may not change, but their hearts will open to receive from a fair teacher. They then can realize that not all members of a group behave the same way. This insight can be the start of building a new mindset that lets students receive from others.

2

✦

Access

I BELIEVED THAT I would always have to fight for what I wanted. My parents had seventeen children, and for a time, no fewer than twelve lived at home in a six-room wooden house with three bedrooms (one for the girls, one for the boys, and one for my parents), a kitchen, a sitting area, and a living room. We fought to sit in a chair at the table or to sleep in a special place in the bed. On Sunday, my mother fixed a special meal that always included fried chicken. We loved fried chicken. I still love it. My parents could afford only one chicken for the family, so if you did not get your plate as soon as Mother put the food on it, someone would grab the chicken off your plate. I cried a few Sundays, and others cried too. At Christmas, we got a few toys to share and fought over the right to play with them. Most of the time, the one who cried the loudest or took a toy and ran was the one who got to play with it.

If we went to pick blueberries or blackberries, we had to fight off mosquitoes and other insects. When we topped tobacco, we had to kill big green worms to finish the job. When we picked cotton, we had to look out for the cockleburs that stuck to our clothes and pricked our skin. When we picked grapes, we had to watch for spiders. When we rode to the fields in the bed of the truck, we fought for a good place to sit. I liked sitting on the side.

Grandmother's house was the drawing card for watching TV on Sundays, the only one in the family for a long time. Our cousins came too. Most of the time, we arrived last because we always had work to do. We had to fight to watch a favorite show or for a place to sit where we could see the TV. In the church we attended, sitting space was limited. The grown-ups sat on the benches, and if the church was full, we had to stand.

My life was full of fighting and contention. I thought I had to fight for everything. When I started school, I carried that mindset with me. I attended a neighborhood school, and most of the children thought they had to fight

3

for everything, just like I did. We did not hit or throw punches, but we did our share of arguing and threatening. I had to be aggressive with my siblings to get a piece of chicken. I had to be aggressive picking berries and topping tobacco. I had to be aggressive at Grandma's house to see the TV. Why would school be different?

Children who grow up fighting for what they want, continue to fight when they come to school. They fight because they believe they must. Fighting can manifest as stubborn arguing, bullying, pouting, talking back, crying, threatening, or insisting on their way. These children have not learned the art of negotiation; they take what they want. I really did not want to fight. Fighting is stressful, and it saps energy. What many children want is to have things available to them without them having to fight. I just wanted a piece of chicken without someone taking it before I could get to my plate.

Students living in poverty are often tagged as troublesome, dishonest, dumb, and lazy. They have to prove their innocence and ability before they get access to some educational opportunities. The opposite is true for some other students, who teachers presume are innocent and able. They get access to most places and educational opportunities without having to prove anything. All students deserve access to places and educational opportunities without some kind of proof.

I once worked at a high school with more than eighteen hundred students, 65 percent of whom were white, and 35 percent nonwhite. White students usually dominated the honor roll, the honor society, and the Beta club; they were the junior marshals and the junior scholars. The choral program (which required an audition), student council, tennis team, swim team, and cheerleading squads were overwhelmingly white. A few nonwhite students found their way into the International Baccalaureate, advanced placement, and honors classes.

Nonwhite students often complained of being selected out of those organizations and clubs or tracked out of challenging academic courses. They thought they did not have the same level of access as white students. This impression could have resulted in low self-esteem, negatively impacting motivation in the school setting, or fostered anger among nonwhite students who thought they must fight for access.

Martha is a compelling example of access. Martha was a tenth grade student who happened to be biracial. The school district had completed a multimillion dollar natatorium to accommodate a swim team. Martha was very excited about the possibility of being a member of this new team. She had been a competitive swimmer since the eighth grade and was hopeful she would earn a spot on the team. The day of tryouts finally arrived and Martha was anxious to show the judges her swimming skills. The next day, the names of the students who made the team was posted. When Martha checked, her name was not on the list. She was heartbroken and complained the only reason she did not make the team was because she was a minority and the only minority who competed. I encouraged her to try again next year. Martha said she would not compete again because she was convinced the outcome would be the same.

Access is a powerful tool in eliminating the urge to fight. Students from poverty need access to teachers who help when needed or asked. They want access to counselors when they need to talk. They need access to the healthy meals they may not get at home. They need access to a challenging curriculum that encourages engagement, to fieldtrips and virtual tours, and to a warm and accepting learning environment. They need access to teachers with high expectations who will hold them accountable, set high standards, and help students achieve them.

3

✦

Scarcity

I believed there was not enough to go around. My house was hot in the summer and hard to cool even with the windows opened. The winter brought different problems. Our house had no insulation, and there were holes in the walls and cracks around the doors and windows. One large heater sat in the middle of the house, and it did not heat the whole thing. Sometimes the temperature dipped below freezing. My mother made quilts, and we regularly had up to four quilts on the bed at night—and still it was cold. The fire died out during the night, and we got up to a cold house. My father rebuilt the fire, but it took time to heat us up. In the meantime, we stood around, shivering and hugging ourselves, waiting for the heater to get hot.

It seems like we ate pork and beans for breakfast, lunch, and supper frequently. We ate them with grits in the morning and over rice for lunch and supper. Pork and beans were cheap and went a long way. My mother added a can of water to every can of pork and beans to feed more people.

The scarcity of heat in the winter and comfort in the summer and the watering down of cheap food left me thinking there was not enough to go around. Children living in poverty confront the problem of scarcity daily. Some do not have enough clothes. Some do not have enough food. There is never enough money. Many do not have enough love. Some do not have enough positive role models. Some do not have opportunities.

When such children enter school, they bring the "not enough" mindset with them. It shows up in the way they view grades. They think, *Only a few students will make As or Bs, and I know there won't be one for me. Since I won't have a chance at an A or B, I will settle for a C. There aren't enough As or Bs to go around. Just one project will be selected as the best, so mine won't have a chance. I won't put much effort into it just to get second or third place.* Students with that mindset put forth little effort and perform poorly, in effect linking poor performance to the shortage of As and Bs, or a chance to place first. Such students must be encouraged, mentored, tutored, and coached to put forth their best effort before they can see how work determines grades.

Carlos a 12th grade honor student illustrates this point. When Carlos was in the ninth grade, most of his grades were low Ds though his teachers reported he could easily be an honor student if he completed his homework and put forth more effort in class. I discussed this with Carlos, and he said he knew that only a certain percentage of the class would make As and Bs. He figured that despite his best efforts, he would not be in that percentage. He was surprised when I told him his teachers believed he could be an honor student. Although he was not convinced that increased effort would translate into higher grades, he committed to working harder because he wanted to attend college. He stayed after school for tutoring three days each week with a mentor to get extra help. By the end of the year, his grades in most subjects were As and Bs.

When students believe everything is scarce, including high grades, school performance will reflect this belief. These students can benefit from encouragement and individual attention. For Carlos, having a mentor who provided tutoring helped him improve his grades and demonstrated that effort does make a difference. A turning point for Carlos was when his teachers voiced their concern about his progress due to a lack of effort and sought a solution.

4

✦

Protest

I BELIEVED I HAD the right to be angry about the hand dealt to me. I remember this incident as if it happened yesterday. We were at the tobacco barn about a hundred yards from Mr. Ed's house, preparing the tobacco for curing. We could see what was going on around his house. The day was very hot, with a bright summer sun. At about 11:00 AM, Mr. Ed's wife and daughter came out of the house wearing bathing suits and sunglasses. Each carried a lounge chair under one arm and a glass of water in the other hand. They staked out a place in the sun and set their water on a small table that was already on the lawn. They opened the lounge chairs, one on each side of the table, and positioned them for reclining. Then they lay back in the lounge chairs. I suppose they were tanning. They stayed outside for quite a while. They never acknowledged our presence—and they did not offer us a drink of cold water.

I was angry. I could not understand why Mr. Ed's daughter, a girl my age, did not have to work like I did. What made her special? My parents did not protest. I did not understand that either. When I railed against his daughter for not helping, my mother ordered me to be quiet. I protested that day by not working as hard as usual because I knew that the situation was unjust.

We had a party line telephone. Several subscribers used one line, usually three parties. Private lines did not exist for us. Any party on a particular line could use the telephone any time someone else was not using it. You lifted the receiver to find out whether the line was in use. If someone else was on the line, you apologized politely and hung up, and you checked again later. If they were still on, they typically gave you an idea how long they would be on the phone. If it was an emergency, most people relinquished the line immediately. We shared a line with Mr. Ed. Dealing with him was different.

My parents made it clear that if Mr. Ed, his wife, or his daughter wanted to use the phone, we were to hang up immediately. I usually obeyed, but I finally decided to show him who was in control. I was on the phone the night after I had watched his wife and daughter sunbathe. Mr. Ed picked up and said, "Gal, I need to use the phone."

"Yessir! I will be right off," I said. Mr. Ed hung up.

A few minutes later, he picked up again. "Gal, I told you I had to use the phone."

Again I said, "Yessir! I will be right off." We went through the ritual four times. I could tell he was angry, but I did not care. In fact, I took enormous satisfaction from it. I knew if my parents found out, they would kill me, but that did not seem to matter. I just wanted Mr. Ed to know how much I resented being treated like a slave.

Mr. Ed lived about five miles from us. A few minutes after our last exchange, he was in the yard, blowing the horn for my father to come out. I peeked out the window and saw his blue truck. I told my cousin on the other end of the line I had to go and hung up. I went back to the window and watched my father talk with Mr. Ed. Soon Mr. Ed left, and my father came back into the house and called me to him. He was uncommonly calm.

"I told you if Mr. Ed ever wants to use the phone, hang up. Don't let that happen again." My father walked away. I thought, *That's all he is going to say. Is he not going to spank me?* He wasn't upset at all. It was though he was saying, "Yes! You did something I couldn't do." I was grateful that my father gave me permission to protest the way Mr. Ed treated us. I realized that night how badly my father must have wanted to do it. From then on, I let Mr. Ed have the phone if he wanted it. I respected my father and was grateful for the respect he showed me.

When children live in poverty or situations where they feel mistreated and powerless, they get angry. When they see their family treated the same way, their anger intensifies. When they see their neighbors treated with disrespect, their anger may be explosive. They will find some way to protest, even risk getting into trouble with authority. They reach a point when they don't care about the consequences. They just want revenge. Sometimes, their methods are self-destructive.

The anger some children bring to school may show up as noncompliant, oppositional, abrasive, opinionated, or defiant behavior that ends in suspension or expulsion. When there are no medical, physiological, or psychological reasons for those behaviors, they may be registering a protest—against the work, the expectations, rules they see as unfair, treatment of other students and themselves, consequences, favoritism, or their own powerlessness. Students who protest want their anger acknowledged and validated. Even it is unjustified and misguided, they still want it acknowledged. If not, they will protest until someone takes notice. When I rebelled about Mr. Ed and the telephone, my father did not protest my protest. His reaction was powerful and empowering to me. I felt I could do something about the way people treated me or my family. Many teachers make a fatal error dealing with protesting students: they protest the student's protest. They get angry and show it. Some teachers see the protest as a personal attack. If my father had scolded me—and I expected him to—he would have propagated more anger. I would have been angry with Mr. Ed, the offender, and my father, my defender. I would have felt powerless to defend my dignity. Sometimes students just want an acknowledgement and the okay to defend their dignity.

Teachers can acknowledge and validate student anger. That may require talking with the student outside of class, though sometimes the protest can be dealt with in class or some similar situation. The school counselor can also talk to students who protest. Teachers who address anger immediately cut the incubation short and will not need an administrator.

A student named Shemekia provides an example of this behavior. Because she was angry, one day she walked out of class without permission. When I asked why, she said she was tried of the teacher playing favorites and making her look bad in front of her friends. I asked her to explain. When she asked questions, she said, the teacher often made demeaning comments like, "You should have learned this in middle school" or, "If you were paying attention, you would know the answer." Shemekia told the teacher how those comments made her feel in front of her classmates. The teacher neither apologized nor indicated she would stop making them.

She also felt the teacher handled discipline unfairly. She let some students talk at inappropriate times without consequences, but others got referrals. She was among the referred. That day the teacher made a demeaning comment in response to her question, and Shemekia had taken all she could. She walked out of the classroom without permission to protest the teacher's behavior and what she perceived as disrespect and unfair treatment. The teacher was upset and referred her to the assistant principal with all the details.

Although the teacher agreed only partially with Shamekia's account of the situation when I had a conversation with him, he recognized that intervention was needed to prevent future incidents of this type. The teacher scheduled a conference with Shamekia and her parents to discuss the matter and to suggest appropriate actions Shamekia should take to resolve such issues if they occur again.

Some students need help learning how to protest without getting into trouble. The school counselor can give them tips and help them acquire new responses. Negative comments, especially in the presence of peers, embarrass students. Making negative comments to students increases the possibility of them becoming angry. Students will generally respond positively when they feel they are being treated fairly and with respect.

5

◆

Entitlement

I BELIEVED I WAS entitled. In Trio, the majority of black people were poor. At least, That's how I saw it as a child. Black people work in the fields. Many black people, especially elderly black people, have less than a tenth grade education. Some black people still do not have indoor plumbing or running water. White people have it all—indoor plumbing, nice houses, running water, and education. And it appears they do not have to work in the fields.

I could not reconcile the two different lifestyles, the way the two races lived in the same community. I could not explain it, but I felt that somehow white people had set the system up that way. After all, white people seemed to have all the advantages. I don't know if I thought I was justified in the way I felt. All I knew was that I felt cheated, and that somebody owed me something. I felt I was entitled to more than I was getting. Most black people felt the same way, so they embarked on a mission to even things up.

This quest led them to the white community. Black people found it difficult, if not impossible, to get what they thought they were entitled to. Apprehensive and remembering their history, they acquiesced. But their quest for justice demanded remedy. Unable and fearful of demanding remedy from white people, they turned to themselves and other black people.

They borrowed money they did not repay, money they felt they had earned only to have white people hold it back. One way or another, they got what they thought was due them. They snubbed other blacks who had less than they did. Money elevated their status and stature in their own eyes and, they believed, the eyes of other black people. They borrowed things and did not return them. Those things represented the hard work for which they were not compensated. Women left their houses unclean and unkempt and said they were tired after working all day in a white woman's house. After all, can a woman be expected to take care of two households? She is entitled to some rest, and so her own house falls into dirt and disrepair. They yell and beat their children because they had a hard day and got neither respect nor due compensation. They slept late on Saturday and refused to work on Sunday because they thought they had given enough. The more they thought about being disenfranchised, the less enthusiastic they were about the quality of their work.

The entitlement phenomenon occurs in many different poverty situations. The child who grows up in the inner city sees the hard work his family does, though nothing seems to change. Many black and poor people clean houses for white and rich people, work for less, are uneducated, and live in lamentable conditions. They have a sense of entitlement just like the poor blacks in rural farming communities. When black people become dissatisfied with their plight, they turn to the white community. The same scenario plays out. They are reluctant to demand fair and equal treatment. After all, white people write their checks. But their quest for justice demands remedy. So they turn to themselves and their people for the remedy. In some cases, they riot, though not in the offenders' community. They riot at home. They destroy and take from themselves in the name of justice and entitlement. In some cases, they take from the welfare system, thereby calling their dignity and character into question. A cycle of deceit and helplessness their children will likely imitate. They may think they are destroying part of the white man's system and thereby forcing him to spend money to repair it. They may see the expense as a kind of indirect payment, but payment nonetheless. Yet they cannot escape the fact that the destruction devalues them as a human being and moves them farther back in the economic line.

In the name of entitlement, students take from themselves and their fellow black students. Schools and classrooms are competitive places. Children in poverty must compete with the children of wealth. Black students know the struggle between blacks who have and blacks who have not. They behave the way anyone who thinks they have been cheated of an entitlement behaves. They take from themselves and other black people. They put forth minimum effort, blaming discrimination and unfair grading practices. They complete fewer assignments than other students do. They seek favors or second chances. The teacher owes them something because they have always been treated unfairly. They ostracize black students who work hard and make good grades. They accuse them of acting white.

How does the entitlement mindset reveal itself in the classroom? Usually such students expect favors, breaks, or pity. Yes, they have had difficult lives. While they deserve an opportunity to learn, develop, and grow to make their lives better, self pity and low expectations cripple them. Sandra's experience illustrates the sense of entitlement. She was upset when she got her report card. She blamed her grades on the teachers' lack of understanding. She was a high school student with two small children. She worked part-time to provide nonessentials. She received state and federal assistance but complained it was not enough for entertainment and dining out.

She completed only certain assignments, was often tardy, and was usually unprepared for class. She was failing most of her courses. Her teachers said she was often disruptive and sometimes refused to follow instructions. When I spoke with Sandra, she lamented being a single mother, having to work, and having to meet her teachers' excessive expectations. She thought they should show more compassion and let her do less work.

Sandra's behavior and work ethics improved significantly after a conference with her mother, social worker, and teachers. The social worker talked with her supervisor and got her work hours reduced. Her mother agreed to taking care of the baby a few hours each evening to allow Sandra to complete homework. Sandra stayed after school on the days she did not report to work for tutoring with her teachers. Her behavior gradually improved and her grades were C's and D's.

The powerful sense of entitlement is born of poverty. Some students think they are entitled to good grades even when they do not earn them. Teachers can help students confront this mindset by demonstrating repeatedly that hard work earns good grades. They can also provide assistance to help students succeed.

6

✦

Second-Rate

I BELIEVED SECOND-HAND CLOTHING was all I could ever hope for. Growing up, I had two older sisters and a host of female cousins. My mother made much of our clothing, and a lot passed down from my sisters or my cousins. My sisters passed their clothes to me after they outgrew them. They often needed mending but were in good enough condition to wear to school. I passed my clothes down to my younger sisters if they were not worn too badly or torn beyond repair. My cousins passed their clothes down to us when they outgrew them or just did not want them any longer. I did not own lots of clothes, and those I had were usually not stylish. Other students snickered, pointed, and giggled. I knew they meant me, though they never admitted it when I confronted them. My clothes were not always pressed. I did not try to make them look nice or color coordinate them. I just put them on, and that was that. I really did not care.

My parents raised hogs, cows, and chickens. They killed a hog and a cow to obtain enough meat to last during winter. They cleaned the intestines (chitterlings) and cooked the feet, liver, and head immediately. My mother cooked the chitterlings separately from the rest and used the liver and head to make a hog-head cheese or hash. She fed us the liver the next morning, fried with gravy over it.

We ate the whole hog: liver, head, and intestines. These were not the choicest cuts. I thought only poor black people ate them. I have to admit, while they did not look inviting, they tasted good. My mother is a great cook. We ate them because my parents could not afford to throw anything away. We had to eat second rate.

Many children growing up in poverty have to settle for second best for a lot of the time. Their parents often shop at thrift stores or flea markets. They live in second-rate neighborhoods in second-rate housing. They attend second-rate schools and are treated like second-rate citizens by many. They use second-rate transportation. Their parents work second-rate jobs. They often receive second-rate medical attention.

In the classroom, a second-rate attitude shows up in the way students approach work. They are accustomed to second-rate things, so they may not understand what first-rate looks, feels, or tastes like. The work they produce is acceptable to them and would be acceptable to others in their environment, but many teachers grade it as second-rate. Some teachers say the child is lazy and unmotivated to do good work. Others may accuse the child of rushing and working haphazardly. In fact, the child may have spent many careful hours on the work. Parents often comment on how hard their children work.

Melissa was a tenth grade student and my counselee. Reviewing her records, I noticed that her standardized tests scores were high, and she made mostly As in coursework. Yet she decided to take mostly technical preparatory courses. This confused me since she had expressed an interest in attending a four-year college. When I asked why she was not taking college preparatory courses, she said she did not feel she could do the work—and her teacher recommended technical preparatory courses. After a conference with her parents, I moved her into college preparatory courses. She completed the courses successfully and graduated with a 3.35 GPA.

Assumptions close doors. When teachers make assumptions about a student's effort, they preclude exploring the reasons why the student's work is not first-rate. Teachers can monitor their own behavior to be sure they are consistently fair and ensure that all students have access to the same opportunities. Ultimately, students decide whether they will take advantage of the opportunities, but teachers should not assume they won't cease opportunities when they are presented.

7

❖

Escape from Stress

SCHOOL WAS IN SOME ways a welcome relief from stress; it was a place to socialize, eat well, and escape from work. Stress at home was high and constant. There was always work to do in the house and on the farm. Around the house, I cooked, scrubbed floors, swept the yard, washed clothes by hand, and took care of my younger siblings. I helped my mother can fruit and vegetables, burn trash, cut wood, clean the house, wash walls and ceilings, and iron clothes. We had no running water, washing machine, or electric stove.

I worked on the farm just as hard. My parents planted tobacco, cotton, corn, wheat, and cucumbers for income. They also planted large seasonal gardens. My jobs included planting, weeding, hoeing, picking cucumbers, canning, stringing tobacco, preparing dried tobacco for the market, cleaning the barns and pack house, and picking cotton.

When I was at school, schoolwork was not a priority. I had worked hard and wrestled with enough negatives before I got to school. School was my refuge. I looked forward to seeing my friends, eating a meal at a table, and relaxing. I usually went to class without the materials I needed and did minimally passing work. My work ethic was different in only one class, about which more later. I completed few homework assignments. I had neither the time nor the energy. The teachers did not penalize me for not having my homework. My parents urged me to finish schoolwork and homework, but they needed my help keeping farm and home. I had no choice. My parents thought I could be a good student and do my work at home too. I did not see how I could do both. I decided that school was a haven.

School is not a priority for many students living in poverty. Often the circumstances of their lives leave them with serious stress. They confront hardship continuously. Some work a full-time job to help the family. Others may be their siblings' main caretakers. Some have the responsibility of caring for an alcoholic or addicted parent. Many live in substandard housing in crime-ridden neighborhoods and rarely have access to health care. Some walk the streets and stay out until late because they are unsupervised. Many live with a single parent and lack a male role model at home. A high percentage of children from single parent homes do not know their fathers. Some children juggle many such issues simultaneously. When they come to school, they are more tired than most other children. They are physically and emotionally drained.

Michael shows us the impact of exhaustion on school performance. The first few weeks of school, Michael came to class and immediately put his head on the desk. His teacher asked him repeatedly to sit up and finish his work. He tried to comply, but after a few minutes, his head was back on the desk. Frustrated, the teacher talked with me because she did not know how to get him to do his work.

I talked with Michael about his life. He had to care for three younger siblings until his mother got home from work at midnight. One was severely mentally handicapped and required constant attention. He did not live in a safe neighborhood, and at times he and his siblings spent most of the evening huddled together in a corner of the room or in a closet, listening to gunfire, police sirens, and ambulances. After his mother came home, he started his homework but soon fell asleep. He said he was tired all the time and worried about his siblings' safety in his neighborhood.

Michael was scheduled for a class each period during the day. I suggested he drop one class for a study hall the first period of the day. The study hall would provide him an opportunity to complete homework, finish any incomplete class assignments, and to sleep if needed. I told Michael's teacher that his family responsibilities included providing care for his siblings at night. The intensive care required by of one of his siblings and his duty to guard their safety in an unsafe neighborhood, often left him exhausted. I did not discuss specifics as I promised Michael, but encouraged Michael to have a detailed discussion with his teacher. I asked his teacher to allow, when possible, additional time for Michael to complete assignments and to discreetly awaken him if he falls asleep. The teacher agreed. Michael is completing more work but is not finishing all of it. He still dozes off in class, but less frequently.

The importance of a positive relationship between students and teachers cannot be overemphasized. Teachers who take the time to get to know their students often understand their plight and can devise a plan to help. They can make adjustments in assignments, such as reducing homework but getting more completed. Caring and nurturing teachers offer an empathic ear and become the child's advocate and mentor. They also can connect students with appropriate school and community resources.

8

✦

Discretionary Learning

SCHOOL ATTENDANCE WAS EXPECTED and enforced. Learning at school, however, was left to my discretion. Only one class was different. My parents insisted I go to school. The laws were on the books, but in Trio, no one would have said anything if I did not go. I showed up most days, looking forward to socializing and relaxing. No teacher ever referred me to the principal for not doing my work. Most of them let me laugh and talk in class, but I was never referred for disturbing a class. They asked about my homework but did nothing when I did not have it. They shrugged their shoulders and moved on to the next student. My teachers never called my parents to report my minimal effort. If I didn't complete assignments, my parents rarely knew it. It was as though my teachers did not expect much from me. Looking back, I suspect I was a good test-taker. How else could I have graduated?

Yes, I was tired. But I wonder—if the teachers had shown an interest in me, would things have been different? It takes only one caring adult to make a difference. For me, that caring adult came along in a tenth-grade algebra class. My teacher thought I was smart. He called on me to answer questions. He usually chose me to work problems on the board. Most of the time, I got them right. He even let me teach the class a few lessons. I completed all the assignments. I earned a better grade in this class than my other classes. I had no problems with inappropriate talking or laughing. He did not assign homework, but if he had, I would have found a way to do it. He bragged about me to my father, and that made us both proud. From then on, my father thought I was smart too.

Any teacher can be the caring adult a child needs. My algebra teacher saw my potential and provided opportunities for me to see it too. I did not want to let him down. He thought I was smart, and I wanted to keep it that way. I never wanted him to think he had made a mistake about me. I worked hard to make sure that did not happen. When I took a course to learn about gifted children, I was pleasantly surprised to learn that many experts in the field believe that all children are gifted. *How* they are gifted is the question. Eric, a special education student classified as *educable mentally handicapped*, was fourteen years old when I taught him. His secondary classification was *emotionally handicapped*, and the school psychologist called his behavior autistic-like.

Eric had a remarkable memory. His favorite thing was to memorize the *TV Guide* and write the contents of the magazine on paper—with every word correctly spelled and every entry just right—something unusual for an *educable mentally handicapped* student.

If somebody asked about the contents of the *TV Guide*, Eric's responses were often irrelevant and inappropriate. In the classroom, he could read and spell words at the seventh grade level, but his comprehension was poor. Memory was his gift. For Eric—and other students like him—the question was not *whether* he was gifted, but *how*.

It makes a difference when teachers recognize and honor their students' gifts. When teachers highlight their gifts, students work hard to make the teacher proud. The drive to impress teachers translates into higher achievement.

A case in point: Asha rarely completed homework, ignored class work, and never finished a project. Her teacher never called her parents or counselor, and Asha never discussed her lack of progress and effort with anyone. She came to school regularly—her parents made sure of that—but she had decided not to work at school, and no one at her school intervened. Unfortunately, Asha did not return to school after her eleventh grade year citing her lack of credits. I wonder what would have happened if someone had taken steps to encourage Asha to work harder in school? I also have some lingering questions about whether she was gifted in some way and if her gift went unnoticed and were not recognized by others.

Many students are in school only because their parents make them comply with federal or state laws. Some of them learn to work hard and focus on learning because some adult cares. One caring adult is all it takes. When students are not working in school, teachers should intervene by involving parents, talking with a school counselor, or insisting students complete assignments. It is also important that gifts and talents students bring with them be identified and recognized.

9

✦

Haphazard Assembly

My mother never cooked with a recipe. She estimated everything, and most of the time she was exactly right. She did not use measuring tools or gadgets. She just decided how much salt to shake into the pot, how much pepper, until it looked about right. The only measuring she did was with her index finger. When she cooked rice, her index finger determined the right amount of water. No matter how much rice was in the pot, the amount of water was critical. Water above the rice up to the second knuckle of the index finger made a perfect pot of cooked rice. When women in Trio shared dishes, they talked about the ingredients but not how much of each ingredient was needed. They bought the ingredients and cooked by trial and error. Dishes varied, depending on who cooked them. One cook might use more of one ingredient than the next. I use some measuring gadgets today, but I still cook rice the way my mother taught me. I still estimate the salt, pepper, and other seasonings. I still add and take away, even when I use a recipe.

My mother did not use patterns to make our clothes. She cut the material by looking at another garment or by instinct. They were not exactly factory made. She used no pattern to make a quilt. She knew what she wanted, and she made it. My father did not read the instructions when he wanted to build or repair something. He built or fixed by trial and error. The result did not always look the way he wanted, but it usually served its purpose. When my mother planted flowers in the yard, she picked a spot she liked and planted. She followed no system or pattern.

I learned how to do many things by trial and error. My parents did not teach us step-by-step methods. I did not learn to start with the end in mind. I had to learn about processes and procedures. I also had to learn how to organize things. I did not have a clue. Everything around me was disorganized. I thought things were supposed to be that way. Most houses and yards in Trio were junky, with things out of place, and my house was no exception. Things around the house and in the house were haphazard—a missing nail, a partially hung curtain, a torn bedspread.

Many children growing up in poverty live in disorganized, junk-filled houses and neighborhoods. A lot of what is around them is in disarray—broken down cars hiked up on blocks, trash thrown everywhere. Clothes are jumbled in piles—rarely hung up in closets. Old papers and magazines are stacked in corners. Broken toys and whatnots litter homes and yards. The furniture is chaotic.

When these children come to school, they try to replicate their home environment, the environment in which they are most comfortable. They plop their backpacks onto the floor or in the aisles. They stuff supplies into their book bags. They turn in sloppy, incomplete, and wrinkled homework written on soiled paper. They cannot locate things they swear they have. They lose things easily. They depend on others to take notes or get assignments. When they write, their thoughts are disorganized. They leave out words or leave sentences incomplete. They hear only part of the instructions before they start to work, since they think they can do without instructions. They bet on the trial-and-error method.

Many children living in poverty do not understand processes or patterns. They have to be taught. They have to learn that most people cook by a recipe. They have to learn that building things right requires blueprints. They have to learn that good writing is a step-by-step process. They have to learn that following steps usually produces an acceptable product and eliminates continuous redoing. They have to learn organizational skills. Children living in poverty have a hard time keeping their belongings organized, since they often live in a disorganized environment. Their thoughts are often just as disorganized and process-free as their environment. What you live, you become.

Teachers where I once worked as a counselor complained endlessly about a particular student. Calvin was a nice young man whose lack of organizational skills and inability to follow directions frustrated them. His assignments were often completed poorly because he did not follow directions. Processes and procedures meant little to him. He rushed to finish assignments and often missed important steps or failed to include critical information. He regularly turned work in on wrinkled or soiled paper. His cubby was usually untidy, and he had a hard time locating what he needed. He wrinkled materials when he shoved them into his cubby or his desk. His teachers said he was bright but did not understand the need to follow a process to complete school tasks. For Calvin, haphazard work was the norm. A visit to his home helped me understand why. Calvin's organizational skills improved and he followed directions better, the more teachers provided step-by-step instructions, limited the number of instructions given at once, insisted he turned in work on clean paper, and demonstrated how to organize materials in his desk.

I recommend patience with such children. They really do not understand processes or organization. They must learn process and procedures are essential to performing well in school. Insightful and caring teachers do not penalize students for not knowing; rather, they teach the skills and knowledge students need.

A constructivist learning approach[5] that gives students the freedom to construct their own knowledge can be beneficial and supports the students' need to be in control. Constructivist learning encourages students to use or build upon old knowledge. This gives them an opportunity to honor their culture and other social aspects. It also empowers them to seek alternative methods to complete assignments, which in turn fosters responsibility. Constructivist learning also teaches and sharpens the process or procedural skills many students lack and satisfies their need to be active participants in the learning process.

---

5   Bencze, *Constructivism*, (pages 1–4).

10

✦

Options

I GREW UP BELIEVING there were few options. Trio had no medical facility. The nearest hospital or health department was twenty miles away. If we got sick, my parents usually medicated us with home remedies. There was no fire department. In case of a fire, neighbors depended on each other. Eating out was not possible: there were no restaurants. Many people walked most places, even long distances.

Financial resources were scarce. Farm work was the main and sometimes the only source of money for some. The money they earned in the spring and summer was gone by the fall. They made less than minimum wage on the farms. If they were sharecroppers, they often ended the farm year deeper in debt. Family vacations or recreation were out of the question. Children amused themselves playing games and inventing toys. I remember traveling sixty miles from home only once when I accompanied my father to Charleston. With me in tow, he took a woman and her daughter to visit her husband in the veterans' hospital. That was the first time I had a burger and milkshake at a Burger King. It was good! I did not eat at a Burger King or travel that far from home again until I went to college.

The cost of living was high. The closest large grocery store was quite a distance away. Families without cars were at a disadvantage. Many families had to shop in Trio and pay higher prices. Other families paid someone to drive them miles to the supermarket. Some mothers made their kids' clothes. They did not have the money or a way to get to department stores in a nearby town.

School resources were inadequate and limited. Schools lacked adequate facilities, appropriate materials, and properly trained teachers. School buildings were in disrepair. Science labs were discussed but never built. Textbooks were second hand, outdated, and tattered. They came second hand from well-funded schools. Students shared books because supply never met demand. From first through twelfth grade, I never had a new book. Supplementary materials were nonexistent. There was no funding for field trips.

Students living in poverty have limited options. Their parents pay higher prices at corner stores for convenience or credit. Many students attend schools with poorly prepared teachers and school buildings in disrepair. Funds for materials and field trips at those schools are meager. If the students eat out, they eat at fast food joints or neighborhood restaurants. Some families have no transportation of their own. They walk, catch a cab, or beg a ride. Most parents work for minimum wage and need all they earn for rent, food, or clothing. There is little money left for family vacations or recreation. Students from such families have little experience in other environments. Some have never been a hundred miles from home. The world is a big place, yet they have only seen their own neighborhoods.

I did not think in terms of options. I thought that what I saw and what I had access to was all that was available to me. I lived in a small world with few options. I was not exposed to different environments or lifestyles. Many students living in poverty have limited exposure to the world beyond their homes. They do not see the world in terms of options because they do not know options exist. Their minds are conditioned to expect and accept little. They bring with them to school a limited-options mindset that dictates their interaction with the learning environment. As a result, some students ask fewer questions and understand less. Their mindset stifles lofty dreams and individual aspirations. They rarely aspire to high academic performance, advanced courses, high SAT/ACT scores, or college. Later few will own homes or businesses; few will travel.

Sammy illustrates the issue of options poignantly. Early in the first semester of his senior year, I met with Sammy to discuss post-secondary plans. I was expecting to hear Sammy list his college choices because of his grades and the college preparatory courses he completed. Instead, he informed me of his decision to join the Marines because he did not have money to pay for college and his parents encouraged him to enlist. His parents both worked but earned only enough money to pay the bills, buy food, and purchase clothing for him and his five siblings. After a lengthy discussion, Sammy commented on his dream of attending college. We discussed scholarships and financial aid. I encouraged him to take the college entrance exam and apply to several colleges. The School Counseling Department provided him with fee waivers for the exam and the applications fees. Few months later, Sammy received acceptance letters from the colleges. His exam score and GPA qualified him for some state scholarships and his final financial aid packet covered most of his tuition and fees. Sammy was excited about having this option being aware that he would need to work to earn spending money. Teachers can help students by encouraging them to ask questions. An inquiry-based curriculum can show students a world of options and often goes beyond the classroom. Teachers can advocate for comprehensive career development programs that open up new worlds for students living in poverty. Many of these students need help identifying their gifts and talents. They must learn about career options and determine the level of education required. Caring teachers challenge students to enroll in higher-level courses and support them, perhaps with tutoring. Insightful teachers move students from a world of few options to a world of unlimited possibilities. To do that, teachers must believe students have the capacity.

11

✦

More Suggestions

THIS CHAPTER OFFERS SUGGESTIONS based on my own observation of students living in poverty to help educators work effectively with them. How these students respond in various situations and how they react to particular behaviors will provide clues to what works with them and what behaviors to avoid. Other suggestions are the result of my personal experience of poverty. I also include some of the strategies I developed or reformulated as I researched the subject of poverty.

- Pay as much attention to the affective domain as to the cognitive. Feelings are important. When feelings are ignored, learning suffers.
- Include all students in activities and classroom discussions.
- Insist on students leaving work and storage areas clean and tidy.
- Keep your word. Avoid disappointing students.
- Validate, respect, and recognize students.
- Schedule a time for conversation between teachers and students, and students and students, to facilitate relationship building.
- Examine your own personal beliefs and assumptions.
- Be genuine. Students know when you are faking it.
- Expose students to a variety of experiences in and out of class.
- Learn what motivates students, and use what you learn to improve academic achievement.
- Create a class of collaborators rather than competitors (i.e., team-building activities, cooperative learning groups, and group projects).

- Privately provide constructive criticism and praise publicly for a job well done.
- Avoid comparing students with other students. Instill an appreciation for personal growth.
- Avoid posting students' grades.
- Design "built-in" success activities.
- Insist on excellence.
- Build positive relationships with parents and families.
- Provide opportunities for students to brag about accomplishments.
- Use creative ways to praise effort and success.
- Focus on the learning process as much as the outcome.
- Be a resource for students.
- Treat errors as a natural part of any process rather than evidence of failure.
- Emphasize effort and skill, and minimize focus on ability.
- Focus on changing beliefs and attitudes.
- Relate to students on a human level.
- Encourage independence by emphasizing self-reliance and personal responsibility.
- Make assignments that can be completed in small steps. Insist on completion of all steps.
- Set realistic classroom rules and enforce them consistently and fairly.
- Model acceptable behavior when transitioning from one activity to another.
- Use frequent and genuine affirmations. Point out gifts and talents.
- Help students set goals and a timetable for meeting each goal.

12

✦

Behaviors and Feelings

POVERTY HAS A CULTURE that often embraces and supports certain behaviors and feelings. I exhibited many of the behaviors mentioned in this chapter and had most of the feelings. Educators are better equipped to work with students living in poverty when they know and understand the behaviors and feelings of their students. Not only are these behaviors and feelings relevant to poverty, but poverty also contributes to acquiring them.

Behaviors
- disorganized
- does not see how one thing is connected to another
- views personal beliefs and opinions as sacred
- hoards because of fear of future shortage
- transitions from one activity to another often chaotic
- suspicious and distrustful
- avoids becoming too close to others outside the family
- spends a lot of time daydreaming
- shies away when things are difficult
- unfamiliar with setting goals
- likes to stay busy and involved

Feelings
- anger due to perception of unfair treatment rejection due to perceived or real exclusion

- disillusioned due to living with disappointment
- shame due to inordinate amount ridicule and judgment
- feels that few choices are available or permitted
- feels trapped by a perceived system of oppression
- feels disconnected from the larger society
- low expectation for success due to past failures

13

✦

Teacher Perception Is Important

ACCORDING TO JERRY BAMBURG[6], a direct correlation connects teacher perception and student achievement. Consciously or unconsciously, teachers respond differently to children from white, middle-class families. His research suggests that teachers who deal with such children:

- smile more
- lean toward students
- make eye contact more frequently offer more opportunities to learn new materials
- ask stimulating questions
- give more time to respond
- give detailed, informative feedback
- praise success more frequently offer engaging instruction
- emphasize meaning and conceptualization
- pace instruction quickly
- ignore minor infractions, or address them less severely

Teachers need to be aware of their behavior toward students to ensure they treat them equally and provide the same opportunities for classroom success to all. Anything short of this contributes to student failure and leaves students feeling frustrated and hopeless. I remember feeling invisible because my teachers ignored me. I could easily have given up, but my parents encouraged

---

6   Bamburg, *Raising Expectations to Improve Student Learning*, (pages 1–3).

me to stay the course. For some of these children, their teachers may be the only people to whom they can look for encouragement.

14

✦

Keeping Expectations High

MY EXPERIENCE WORKING WITH students living in poverty and with teachers led me to the conclusion that teacher expectations affect student learning. Teachers must demonstrate their belief in students' ability to achieve. When students know their teachers have high expectations of them, they usually meet or exceed those expectations. As a teacher and counselor, I have found the following suggestions helpful in communicating high expectations to students.

- Actions speak louder than words. Actions communicate expectations.
- Communicate to students your belief in their desire to learn.
- Change time, grouping, and teaching methods to accommodate different learning styles.
- Refuse to accept failure as an option.
- Provide a level of assistance likely to result in success.
- Hold students accountable.
- Understand the students' culture and how it affects behavior and attitude.
- Avoid any appearance of ability grouping, which affects motivation adversely.
- Seek input from parents about how they want to be involved. Many parents have their own ideas about parental involvement.
- Stress the importance of effort instead of focusing solely on ability.
- Provide rigorous and challenging work to keep students engaged.
- Strategically offer opportunities for success.

Conclusion

I leave you with these thoughts:

- One person can make a positive difference in a life, so imagine the power of two.
- Knowing that someone loves you enough to provide critical, timely support empowers you to change your life.
- Some negative experiences build resilience.
- Some children need help to understand their level of resiliency.
- Educators are powerful influences in children's lives.
- Given a fair chance, most students succeed.
- Poverty does not have to be the last word on a student's potential for growth and achievement.

I wish you the best as you work with all children to instill confidence and improve academic achievement.

Bibliography

Association of American and Universities, s.v. "Greater Expectations to Improve Student Learning (by Ross. Miller), www.greaterexpectations.org/briefing_papers/ImproveStudentLearning.html (accessed October 24, 2006).

Clearinghouse on Educational Management, s.v., "Expectations for Students" (by Linda Lumsden) www.eric.ed.gov (accessed September 20, 2006).

Early Childhood Research and Practice (ECRP), s.v. "Readiness for School: A Survey of State Policies and Definitions" (by Gitanjalis Saluja, Catherine Scott-Little, and Richard M. Clifford), www.ecrp.uiuc.edu (accessed September 28, 2006).

ERIC Clearinghouse on Elementary and Early Childhood Education, s.v. "Failure Syndrome Students" (by Jere Brophy), www.eric.ed.gov (accessed October 24, 2006).

ERIC Digest, s.v. "Raising Expectations to Improve Student Learning" (by Jerry D. Bamburg), www.eric.ed.gov (accessed October 22, 2006).

Focus Adolescent Services, s.v., "Youth Who Drop Out" www.focusas.com/Dropouts.html (accessed on September 26, 2006).

Ontario Institute for Studies in Education of the University of Toronto, s.v. "Constructivism" (by John Lawrence Bencze), www.leo.oise.utoronto.ca/~lbencze/Constructivism.html (accessed December 9, 2006).

United Health Foundation, s.v. "16th Annual America's Health Rankings Shows Slowing Rate of Improvement after Significant Health Gains in 1990s," www.unitedhealthfoundation.org/media2005 (accessed October 19, 2006). *U.S. Census Bureau*, s.v. "Poverty: 2002 Highlights," www.census.gov (accessed October 19, 2006).

About the Author

Regenia Mitchum Rawlinson, MEd, NCC, NCSC, NBCT, GCDFI, has been an educator for over thirty years. She has worked as a special education teacher, an elementary school counselor, a high school counselor and director, and a district administrator.

Regenia grew up in poverty, and since 1997, she has been sharing her ideas and insights with educators and other professionals to help them understand a mind shaped by poverty and how poverty-mindedness affects academic achievement and behavior. She is a local, state, and national speaker as well as a leader in the areas of culture and school climate and an expert on the topic of poverty.

She earned a BA from Winthrop College and a master's degree from Winthrop University. She lives in South Carolina with her husband David; they are the parents of three adult children.

Made in the USA
Lexington, KY
13 March 2012